MANAGING
PERFORMANCE ANXIETY
IN

TENNIS

Dr Andrew Peden PhD
Clinical Psychologist

Note for Librarians: A cataloguing record for this book is available from Library and Archives Canada at www.collectionscanada.ca/amicus/index-e.html
ISBN 1-4251-2080-6

Printed in Victoria, BC, Canada. Printed on paper with minimum 30% recycled fibre. Trafford's print shop runs on "green energy" from solar, wind and other environmentally-friendly power sources.

Offices in Canada, USA, Ireland and UK

Book sales for North America and international:
Trafford Publishing, 6E–2333 Government St.,
Victoria, BC V8T 4P4 CANADA
phone 250 383 6864 (toll-free 1 888 232 4444)
fax 250 383 6804; email to orders@trafford.com
Book sales in Europe:
Trafford Publishing (UK) Limited, 9 Park End Street, 2nd Floor
Oxford, UK OX1 1HH UNITED KINGDOM
phone +44 (0)1865 722 113 (local rate 0845 230 9601)
facsimile +44 (0)1865 722 868; info.uk@trafford.com
Order online at:
trafford.com/07-0484

10 9 8 7 6 5 4 3 2

Para Alison. Mi Esposa. Te Quiero.

Preface

Do you play tennis? The very fact that you are reading this preface suggests that you do. That you have chosen to browse or buy a book with the title 'Managing Performance Anxiety in Tennis' further suggests that you are interested in the mental or psychological side of the game.

But are you aware that the psychological side of tennis is even more important than good tennis technique? Did you know that it is not forehands and backhands but the psychological side of tennis which differentiates players of roughly equal ability from one another? It is the psychological side of tennis that can make the difference between playing well and playing badly; between winning and losing. Being good at the psychological side of tennis lets players rise to the top of their club league or ladder just as much as it allowed Roger Federer and Maria Sharapova to climb to the top of the world rankings.

Although being aware of and being able to use to your advantage the mental side is important in all aspects of the game, this book is aimed specifically at managing performance anxiety in tennis from a clinical sports psychology perspective. Ask your self these questions: Have you ever found yourself worrying about a game you were due to play? Has that worry made you tense? On court, have you ever felt your breathing becoming laboured, your heart pounding, your legs heavy and butterflies in your stomach? Have thoughts of self-doubt raced through your mind? Have you cursed your inability to play seemingly simple shots, either quietly to yourself under your breath or out loud? In a match, do you ever miss shots that you make consistently in your coaching sessions or practise games? Do you ever double-fault at crucial points in a game? If you have answered 'No' to most of these questions then you are probably not human! Or else Roger or Justine has bought the book also! (Thanks guys). For most of us though, many of these descriptions will sound all too familiar. Would you like to understand more about why you have experienced them? Perhaps more importantly, would you like to do something to prevent them from happening again in the future?

If the answer to any of these questions is 'Yes', then this book is for you. The book is unique in the market. Whilst there are several books to help with the general mental side of the game, none focuses specifically upon managing anxiety in order to help improve tennis performance when it matters most—in a match.

The book is organised into two broad parts. Part one is more theoretical; it explores the meaning of anxiety and stress and explains how anxious thoughts and feelings can lead to anxious behaviour which inhibits performance. It also looks at how individuals differ in their propensity to feel anxiety; and how people respond differently to stressful situations, such as playing in front of an audience—and in tennis, it is important to be aware that the 'audience' may be a single opponent or even our coach.

Part two focuses on specific psychological techniques to manage performance anxiety in tennis in order to improve your game. It is full of practical advice and tips, broken down into different sections to correspond with the somatic (physical), cognitive (thinking) and behavioural (doing) aspects of anxiety. If offers advice on matters such as deep breathing exercises, relaxation training, distraction, positive self-talk, visualisation, body language and coping with pressure. If you read this book and put into practice just one or two of its suggestions, your game will improve; if you practice all of the suggestions, your game will improve further still.

About The Author

Dr Andrew Peden is a Chartered Psychologist and Associate Fellow of the British Psychological Society (BPS). He has an Honours Degree in Psychology, a Masters Degree in Clinical Psychology and a Ph.D. in Health Psychology. He has completed post-graduate trainings in family therapy, group analytic psychotherapy and individual psychodynamic psychotherapy. He works and lives in Manchester, England, where he is in full-time private practise as a Consultant Clinical Psychologist.

Dr Peden provides psychological services to individuals and groups across the age-range and consults to a variety of agencies and institutions; but his greatest interest and passion lies is in the application of psychological theories and techniques to sport in general and tennis in particular. His maxim is that tennis is a sport played on a court but a game played in the mind; his greatest hope for this book is that those who read it will find something in it of relevance and value that they can apply to their unique situation in order to improve their tennis game and move closer to their tennis-playing potential.

For correspondence concerning the book or advice about psychological matters in general, Dr Peden may be contacted by email at: adpeden@aol.com

Acknowledgments

To Alison, my wife and mixed-doubles partner, for her ever-present support and love. To Eve, tennis ace, for her ever-present Positive Mental Attitude. To Stephen Renwick, tennis coach, author and friend, for his ever-present inspiration to write this book.

Contents

PART ONE
ANXIETY

CHAPTER ONE
What is Anxiety?

Chapter Objectives

After reading this chapter you will be able to describe:

How anxiety is universal
The fight or flight response
The symptoms of somatic anxiety
Thoughts associated with cognitive anxiety
How anxiety effects tennis
The vicious cycle of anxiety
Why avoidance is unhelpful

John stands just behind the baseline, waiting to receive serve. He is 5-3 down. He can almost hear his heart beating; he is still trying to catch his breath from the previous point. His shoulders feel stiff; his grip on the racquet feels painfully tight. He has lost the bounce in his feet and the idea of 'split-stepping' is far from his mind.

His mind is racing. He is thinking—'I must win this point or I am going to lose again'. He cannot help remembering and almost reliving in his mind's eye the last two returns of serve, both of which went straight into the net, causing him to groan and shout out loud that he was 'rubbish' as his shoulders slumped and his face grimaced.

John has played this opponent twice before; he lost on

both occasions. This has left him feeling a powerful mixture of embarrassment and anger—he knows he is a technically more gifted player and should be able to beat his opponent quite easily. Not only does he know this, so does everyone else in the club—including his playing partners and coach. He thinks—'I am going to have to tell everyone again that I have lost'.

The serve approaches. At the last moment, flat on his feet, his attention overly narrowed due to his ever-rising anxiety, John misjudges the flight and bounce of the ball. At the last second, he sticks out an arm and manages to make a late and weak connection with the ball, which flies low into the net. Game, Set and Match to his opponent. Again.

John shakes hands at the net and tries to smile, without much success. He congratulates his opponent but thinks to himself, 'I am going to withdraw from the league. Maybe I am not good enough to play competitive tennis. I am a failure. I feel terrible'.

Does this scenario sound at all familiar? I am sure it will to many of you. Would you like to understand why John (or you) has experienced this? Would you like to do something to prevent it from happening in future? If the answer to any of these questions is 'yes', then this book is for you. Read on.

Anxiety

Anxiety and stress are universal, parts of everyday life. We have all felt anxious or stressed at some point—to be anxious is to be human. Indeed, not only is anxiety inevitable, it is a necessary emotion; it can motivate us to do things we might not do otherwise. For example, worrying that we might not do well at something important might motivate us to revise for crucial exams, train harder to get match fit for a big tournament, or simply practice more in order to play better tennis.

However, whilst anxiety is inevitable and at times useful, on occasions it may become dysfunctional—that is, it may interfere with our ability to behave in helpful ways. In this book, I want to distinguish between 'neurotic' anxiety—anxiety that is out of all proportion to real danger—and 'objective' anxiety—anxiety related to a specific situation: in this case, competitive tennis.

Fight or Flight

Anxiety is part of our evolutionary past, as it is for all animals; necessary for survival, anxiety triggers the 'fight or flight' response. That is, in situations of potential danger—real or imagined—anxiety prepares the body to confront or 'fight' the danger or to run away and take 'flight'.

For example, imagine being confronted by a mugger on a dark night. You could either stand your ground and fight him; or you could take flight and run away from the danger. Many people will be familiar with this concept, although perhaps much less aware of the third potential response to anxiety—'freezing', or the inability to act in the face of stress.

The Three Systems: body, mind and behaviour

It is important to recognise and understand that anxiety effects our bodies, our minds and how we act; and that there is a complex and ever-changing interplay between those three systems—the somatic, cognitive and behavioural: how we feel, the ways in which we think and what we actually do when we are anxious. The effects of anxiety on each of these three systems will be considered in turn.

Somatic Anxiety

When we are anxious, regardless of the cause, we experience physical changes or feelings in our bodies. These feelings are triggered by the production of adrenaline in order to meet the demands of the 'fight or flight' response. Adrenaline is a naturally occurring chemical, present in everyone's body. Adrenaline is actually a hormone—a chemical produced in one organ of the body which exerts its effects on other organs of the body. The effects of adrenaline on the body's various organ systems are many, but include:

- changes in the respiratory rate, producing breathlessness and sensations of smothering or choking;

- increased blood flow to the heart, causing palpitations and a pounding heart;

- alterations in blood pressure, leading to feelings of dizziness and light headedness;

- increased muscle tension, causing chest pains, pins and needles, tingling, cramps and headaches;

- excitation of the digestive system and urinary tract producing stomach pains, abdominal distress, nausea, diarrhoea and a frequent urge to urinate;

- alteration of the body's temperature control mechanism or thermostat, causing perspiration, reddening of the skin, hot flushes or cold chills;

- general over-arousal of the nervous system leading to restlessness, tremors and jumpiness.

Cognitive Anxiety

Cognitions are thoughts, beliefs and ideas. An individual's cognitive style is the way in which they typically think about themselves, other people and the world in general. Certain cognitive styles and ways of thinking are strongly associated with anxiety.

The central idea behind the cognitive model of anxiety is that it is not actual events in the external world which cause us to be anxious; rather it is our expectations, perceptions and interpretations of those events which produces anxiety as an emotional reaction.

For example, if we have been in a tennis tournament and under-performed, played badly and lost all of our matches, then the next tournament we enter is likely to trigger memories of our earlier feelings, leading to anxious cognitions, including thoughts of self-doubt and a questioning of our abilities.

When we feel anxious, our cognitions tend to relate to perceptions of danger—either physical (the threat of actual bodily harm) or psychosocial (for example, the loss of self-esteem, the fear of criticism or ridicule). Anxious cognitions commonly include thoughts of apprehension, self-doubt, worry, fear, a sense of impending danger and threat.

These anxiety-related perceptions typically lead to negative automatic thoughts—thoughts which enter or pop into our heads without being reasoned through and are associated with unpleasant emotional feelings. Negative automatic thoughts commonly begin with statements such as, 'I can't......I won't be able to.....I will never......I am a failure....'

Negative automatic thoughts are often underpinned by dysfunctional assumptions or general beliefs about oneself or certain situations, even at times when the individual cannot clearly specify of what it is they are fearful, such as: 'I always fail to....Unless I win people will not like me....

Anything other than 1st place means I am a failure'. Dysfunctional assumptions are typically rooted in childhood experiences, are sometimes difficult to access by conscious thought and particularly triggered at times of stress.

Behaviour: How Stress and Anxiety Effect Tennis

'Stress' is defined as the difference between our perception of the demands placed upon us and our perceived ability to cope with those demands. This definition recognises the importance of the situation but also of the individual and their perception of, beliefs about and attitude to that situation. That is why the exact same situation might be seen as stressful by one person but as a challenge by another—individual psychological differences of the type that will be explored more fully in the following chapter.

If we feel able to cope with the demands placed upon us, then we are unlikely to feel much stress—we believe that we have the resources to cope with the situation in which we find ourselves. Anxiety arises when we perceive the demands placed upon us to be greater than our perceived ability to cope with those demands. This mismatch typically produces fear and anxiety. When both somatic and cognitive anxiety is excessive, they will inhibit performance.

Performance Expectations

In a situation such as a tennis match, it is unlikely that we are going to be under much physical threat (aside perhaps from being hit by a driven ball whilst standing at the net!); but we are likely to be exposed to psychosocial threat, for example threats to our self-image and self-esteem from fear of performing badly, of losing, or being viewed negatively by our opponent or onlookers.

In tennis, if we play an opponent whom we perceive to be far below us in ability terms, then we expect to win easily and we are unlikely to feel much stress or anxiety as a result. Similarly, if we play an opponent whom we perceive to be far above us in ability terms, then our expectations of success will be low—we expect to lose and so we are likely to feel less competitive stress and anxiety.

Stress and hence anxiety is more of a problem when we play someone we perceive to be close to us in terms of ability. Typically, this will be the player a few places above us on the club's tennis ladder; or an opponent within the same division of the tennis league. These matches should, by definition, be close, and therefore a likely cause of tension and anxiety.

Arousal and Muscular Tension

Self-doubt, negative thoughts and worry-laden expectations are likely to trigger certain changes in the body, particularly those involving the autonomic nervous system as the body prepares for what is commonly known as 'fight or flight'. High levels of arousal and anxiety lead to increased muscular tension. As sporting success depends heavily on muscle co-ordination, high levels of anxiety can impede physical performance and cause a player to tighten up and become over-tense.

Muscular tension, even at low levels, can interfere with co-ordination, resulting in poor performance, for example: a poor or incomplete backswing and follow-through with a shot hit either too long and out or too short leaving our opponent an easy attacking winner.

Muscular tension can make our legs feel heavy and our feet 'stick' to the ground, resulting in slow reactions and poor or clumsy footwork, leaving us either too far away or too close to the ball when we swing.

Muscular tension can cause tightness of breath as our breathing becomes too rapid and shallow, meaning that we tire easily, especially after a long rally, after running to the net to meet a drop shot or racing to the back of the court to retrieve a lob.

If the match is close and goes to a tie break or a third set, we may have expended so much unnecessary energy through nervous tension in our muscles that we tire and fall at the crunch points.

The Double Fault

I am sure all of us have experienced at least some of these difficulties. Every player, regardless of ability and experience, will have felt tension in their shoulders and arms whilst serving, especially at important points in the match—30-30 in a game, 4-4 in a set, when serving to close the set or at match point—leading to a serve wide, long, into the net or the dreaded double fault.

Have you noticed how double faults seem most likely to occur at crucial and deciding moments in a match? Have you observed how one double fault in a game can so often lead to two or three in succession? That is the result of muscular tension. The serve is technically the most difficult skill to learn and is often the difference between winning and losing, especially in a game between two evenly matched players. Like any skill, under pressure that which is most difficult, least mastered or most recently learnt is the first to fail.

Negative Automatic Thoughts

Increased anxiety also influences an individual's ability to attend, concentrate, and think clearly and positively. In a tennis match, an anxious player may be prone to a whole series of negative automatic thoughts—that is thoughts or images aroused in the specific on-court situation which predispose that individual to feel anxious. Such thoughts might include:

- 'I missed that serve, therefore I am a rubbish player';

- 'I can feel my arm stiffening up, which means that I won't be able to swing properly';

- 'I can't stop hitting the ball short, my opponent will punish me and I will lose the game and ultimately the match'.

Choking

Professional sportsmen and women are not immune to negative automatic thoughts, somatic arousal, tension and under-performance. In golf, it is called the 'yips'; in other sports, it is sometimes termed the 'jitters; but in tennis, it is referred to as 'choking'. Choking under pressure occurs when a player fails to perform, typically in important situations. For example, Pat Rafter admitted to choking in the Wimbledon final of 2000 when in sight of winning; and Amelie Mauresmo was repeatedly accused by the press of choking in major finals until she managed to win in the Australian Open of 2006.

Rituals

Many sportsmen and women, from recreational to professional levels, engage in superstitious behaviours or rituals. Amongst tennis players, some like to wear their 'lucky' shirt or socks;

male professionals playing in major tournaments sometimes do not shave or cut their hair whilst they are on a winning streak; in a match, some players like to continue serving using the ball with which they won the previous point. Some of these superstitious rituals border on the compulsive. At the extreme but not that uncommon level, some professional players engage in rigid routines throughout their entire pre-match preparation—staying in the same hotel; everyday eating the same meal at the same seat in the same restaurant; watching the same TV show before they leave; listening to the same music whilst being driven by the same driver to the tournament—and so on.

On court, if you look closely you will see players' highly developed rituals for the use of the towel between points; bouncing the ball a set number of times depending on whether it is a first or second serve; and in the chair between games adjusting items of clothing, such as tying and retying their laces.

Whilst these superstitious behaviours may help with focus and concentration and take the player's mind off external distractions, whether or not they know it, one of the major reasons why players engage in these and other superstitious rituals is in order to ward off anxiety.

Whilst at surface level they may seem harmless, the difficulty with these rituals and superstitions is that, for some players, if for any reason they are prevented from engaging in their rituals, their levels of anxiety rise higher and higher and can interfere with their ability to focus upon what really matters and the only thing over which they have any actual control—the game.

Self-fulfilling prophecies

How often have you known in your heart that you are going to double-fault on your second serve? I'm sure this has happened to all of us. How often have you known that even though you were 5-2 up and serving for the game, you would not be able to hold to your serve and your opponent would get back into the match and even beat you?

These are examples of so called 'self-fulfilling prophecies'—variation of negative self-talk that produce muscular tension, inhibit coordination and produce mistakes. Self-fulfilling prophecies can cause the player to focus so much on what *not* to do that they somehow almost forget what they have to do—for example, they become so focused on avoiding double-faulting that they lose all sense of where they should serve.

Avoidance

Because anxiety is typically felt as uncomfortable or unpleasant, it commonly leads to certain behaviours, usually involving avoidance, which act in the short-term to reduce the unpleasant feelings associated with anxiety— for example, 'I will avoid playing him/her again because I was too anxious during the game' or 'I won't play in anymore league matches because I was too anxious and did not perform'.

In the short-term, such avoidant behaviours reduce anxiety; but avoidance breeds more avoidance and in the longer-term avoidance simply reinforces and strengthens the likelihood of anxiety occurring again in a similar situation and is therefore maladaptive and unhelpful. To conquer our fears we need to face up to them in order to learn that they can be overcome and that we have control over our feelings and behaviours.

The table below summarises some of the somatic, cognitive and behavioural consequences of anxiety.

How Anxiety Effects the Body's Thoughts and Behaviours

The Body	Thoughts	Behaviour
Breathlessness	Apprehension	Fight
Palpitations	Doubt	Flight
Dizziness	Worry	Freeze
Light-headedness	Fear	Avoidance
Muscular tension	Impending danger	Poor Coordination
Chest Pains	Threat	Poor Technique
Pins and Needles	Negative Thoughts	Clumsy Footwork
Cramps	-I can't	Easily Tired
Headaches	-I won't be able to	Double Faults
Abdominal distress	-I will never	Choking
Nausea	-I always fail to	
Diarrhoea		
Restlessness		
Perspiration		
Hot and Cold Flushes		

The Vicious Cycle

Heightened bodily arousal, negative automatic thoughts and avoidant behaviour can then set up a 'vicious cycle' in which being on-court, particularly in a competitive match, can trigger bodily sensations of anxiety, negative thoughts and images, leading to an increased perception of psychosocial threat, resulting in heightened autonomic arousal and more negative thoughts, therein physically and mentally inhibiting one's ability to play the game effectively.

This is why so many club players under-perform in competitive situations—they play freely and brilliantly in a 'knock' or social game; but in a ladder or league match always seem to lose to players with much less technical ability.

The diagram below illustrates the links between the somatic, cognitive and behavioural components in the vicious cycle of anxiety.

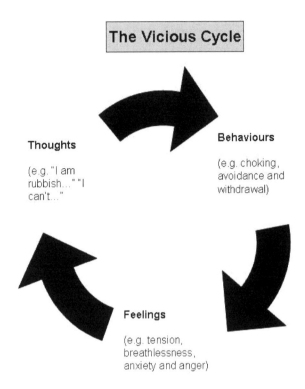

The good news is that you can do something to help reduce your anxiety and increase your performance potential!
Subsequent chapters in this book will show you how. But
firstly we will explore how individual differences, importance and uncertainty, and the presence of an audience can
all create anxiety and effect performance.

CHAPTER TWO
Individual Differences

Chapter Objectives

After reading this chapter you will be able to describe:

The differences between state and trait anxiety

Event importance & uncertainty and anxiety

The effects of an audience on performance

Why some anxiety is helpful

Peter and Eve are both playing in their first official tournaments—the club's annual men's and women's singles events. There are over 30 entrants in each event and this morning is the first round. Everybody has to turn up at 10am and play at least one match. Lots of people—players, coaches and other club members—are milling around. When Peter and Eve begin their matches, there are at least half-a-dozen people watching intently, 15 or more watching occasionally and several dozen casual observers.

Peter feels terrible. From the very first point, his game goes to pieces. He can't return serve, he hits wide or long and misses volleys that he normally plays in his sleep. Every time he hits a poor shot, his body tenses and his muscles tighten more and more. He starts to think about how the onlookers must be regarding him—'How rubbish they must think

I am.' Every time this thought goes through his mind, he performs even worse as he gets caught up in a 'vicious cycle' of negative expectations, physical tension and the behavioural consequences of under performance.

On the next court, Eve is feeling good. From the very first point, her game is positive. She returns serve deep and hard; she approaches the net and volleys a winner. Every time she hits a good shot, she feels loose, agile and energised. She starts to think about how the onlookers must be regarding her—'How good they must think I am.' Every time this thought goes through her mind, she performs even better and sets up a 'virtuous cycle' of positive expectations, optimum physical arousal and the behavioural consequences of good performance.

Personality differences—state versus trait anxiety

State Anxiety

The way we feel at any given moment in a particular situation is known as 'state' anxiety. Competitive state anxiety is a subjective emotional feeling involving heightened arousal of the autonomic nervous system. It varies in intensity from mild tension, apprehension and a sense of inadequacy, to intense fear or even terror.

State anxiety is subjective and consciously felt. It reflects an individual's changing mood—so by definition it is transitory and can change from moment-to-moment during a tennis match. State anxiety is often highest at the beginning of the match, reduces as the player gets into the pace of the game, and increases at certain crucial points, particularly break, set and match points. It falls dramatically after winning.

Trait Anxiety

Whilst state anxiety is ever changing, situationally dependent, prone to much fluctuation across time and situation, 'trait' anxiety is part of an individual's personality and therefore more stable, enduring, wide-ranging and resistant to change. Trait anxiety is the predisposition to perceive a wide range of situations as threatening. The individual high in trait anxiety responds to such circumstances with elevations of state anxiety—that is, they become even more anxious! So, if we typically feel anxious (that is, we have high levels of trait anxiety) and we put ourselves into a situation likely to arouse anxious feelings (e.g. a situation in which we are judged or evaluated—such as a competitive tennis match) then our anxiety levels are likely to be very high indeed and we will feel and experience many of the somatic, cognitive and behavioural consequences outlined in the previous chapter, resulting in significant underperformance.

Not only has psychological research demonstrated that individuals high on levels of trait anxiety experience heightened levels of state anxiety in situations of competition or personal evaluation, such as competitive tennis; it has shown that there is a very close relationship between high levels of trait anxiety and low self-esteem.

Self-esteem is usually defined as the perception the individual possesses of his or her own self-worth that emerges and takes shape as the child develops, differentiating as that individual matures and interacts with significant others. Self-esteem is viewed as a composite of an individual's feelings, hopes, fears, thoughts and views of whom they have been, who they are, and what they might become.

Individuals high on underlying trait anxiety are predisposed to view competitive situations as more threatening than those with low levels of trait anxiety. If they also have low self-esteem, then they will be less confident in competitive situations, in which they will experience heightened bodily arousal and increased negative thinking. Their anxiety levels may be such that they interfere with their performance and ability to play well under conditions of competitive stress. Thankfully, there are ways to counter this potentially destructive combination. One way is to learn to reduce your state anxiety levels. Later chapters in this book will show you how to do this. Another way is to work on improving your self-esteem. This book does not specifically address self-esteem but it almost goes without saying that if you can improve your general self-esteem and feel good about yourself in other aspects of your life (e.g. your social world and relationships with family and friends, your appearance and career) then this will make you feel better about yourself and help reduce your general anxiety levels.

However, with specific reference to the focus of this book—tennis—if you can learn to relax on court and thereby improve your game and chances of winning, then you will feel less anxious whilst playing and consequently better about yourself and your tennis abilities.

This will then help improve your self-esteem as a tennis player and reduce your anxiety—changing a vicious cycle into a virtuous one. This is one reason why even highly anxious people off court can be excellent, winning tennis players on court—they are secure in the knowledge that they can play tennis well, to a high level, and are therefore less likely to feel too much tension in the competitive situation.

Situational Stress

Importance and Uncertainty

Anxiety levels will also be influenced by event importance and uncertainty. As a general rule, the more important a match is to an individual, the more anxiety it will arouse—that is why a 'knock' with a good friend is much less anxiety provoking than a league match; and a first round game is likely to be much less anxiety provoking than a final. Within a game, the more important the point, the more anxious one is likely to feel—with break points likely to arouse the most anxiety. Within a set, as the set draws closer to the end the more anxious and tense one will become—which is why it is so difficult to close a set even when winning comfortably and especially when serving at 5-4 or 6-5.

Also, the less certain the outcome, the more anxiety there will be—which is why it is often much less anxiety provoking to play somebody we perceive to be far below us in ability terms, as we simply expect to win, or to play somebody far better than us, as we expect to lose, than it is to play someone we perceive to be of roughly comparable ability. Playing someone more or less as able as us heightens our level of uncertainty and increases our anxiety and stress levels.

As can be seen from the table below, the most anxiety arousing situation will be when a game is important but the outcome is uncertain—for example, a big tournament against a closely matched opponent, creating a situation of high importance and high uncertainty and therefore high anxiety, contrasting most sharply with a situation of low importance and low uncertainty (for example, a knock with a relative beginner) which should produce in us no anxiety.

Importance, Uncertainty & Anxiety

U N C E R T A I N T Y	H I G H	MEDIUM ANXIETY	HIGH ANXIETY
	L O W	NO ANXIETY	MEDIUM ANXIETY
		LOW	HIGH
		IMPORTANCE	

Social Facilitation Theory

Have you ever noticed how some people perform better in front of an audience and others perform worse? That when playing tennis in high pressure situations whilst being watched by an audience, some players improve their game whilst others play badly or even choke? How does this work? Why are people so different from one another?

Research has shown that individual differences in performance in front of an audience reflect a combination of unique psychological characteristics, interacting with the demands of the situation in which we find ourselves and the presence of other people—the 'audience'. The psychologist Gordon Allport coined the term 'social facilitation' to explain why the presence of an audience improves performance at tasks we have mastered and know well; but the presence of an audience causes under-performance in tasks we have not learned well or which are too complex for us at that stage in our skill development or learning.

This is one reason why the shot we have been working on in coaching for the last few lessons and which has been going well in that situation simply goes to pieces in a match—it is not yet secure enough or sufficiently well-established within our muscle memory to be effective under competitive pressure, especially in front of an audience.

This works in both the body and the mind to effect behaviour. According to the 'drive' theory of social facilitation, the presence of spectators increases arousal such that our bodies become overly aroused, making it difficult to perform newly learnt or complex tasks. This is combined with our cognitive style or way of thinking; being fearful of evaluation, having high trait anxiety and low self-esteem, create a destructive combination that can predispose us to anticipate criticism or even ridicule and therefore perform badly in the presence of an audience.

If you watch people playing tennis at your club, you will I am sure see plenty who miss a couple of shots and then spend the rest of the match trying to avoid playing the shot they have just missed—typically, but not always, the backhand, which is the obvious weakness of most club level players. Whilst at one level this might seem like a reasonable strategy, because it is an avoidant method of coping it is helpful only in reducing anxiety in the short-term; in the long-term it is dysfunctional or unhelpful because the avoided shot will remain weak and an observant or tactically aware opponent will play to it constantly, causing you to make more rather than fewer errors as intended by your attempts at avoidance.

Of course, the concept of 'audience' need not only apply to a group of spectators—few club players will have an audience watch them—it can extend simply to a single opponent or even our coach. Studies have shown that the presence of even an individual spectator or onlooker can either facilitate or inhibit performance, depending upon the individual and the specific situation in which they find themselves.

The inverted-u hypothesis

Psychologists have identified another relationship between anxiety levels and performance—known as the 'inverted-u hypothesis'. Typically, at low anxiety levels there is likely to be a degree of under-performance as the player lacks motivation and is not 'psyched up' enough to perform to the best of their ability—remember, anxiety can motivate us to do things we might not otherwise do, such as practice and remain focused and competitive.

As our level of anxiety increases, our performance increases incrementally. However, if anxiety increases past a certain point, then this will have a negative effect upon performance as over-arousal or too much anxiety and tension will interfere with performance ability. At extreme levels this can even cause 'choking'. This relationship can been seen in the diagram below which shows how poor performance can result from either too little or too much anxiety, with optimal anxiety producing optimal performance.

Graph 1: Anxiety & Performance: the inverted-u hypothesis

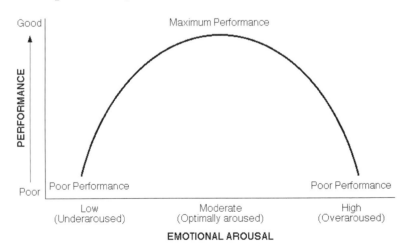

Of course, sports psychology recognises that we are all individuals and there is no 'one size fits all' theory to predict the wide variation that exists between people. However, the inverted-u hypothesis is a helpful model for understanding the relationship between anxiety and performance in a range of sports; detailed knowledge of a player (or oneself) will allow us to plot onto the graph optimal levels of arousal for each individual. The diagram below illustrates the differences between two tennis players—Player 1 and Player 2—using the inverted-u hypothesis.

Graph 2: Individual Differences in Anxiety & Performance

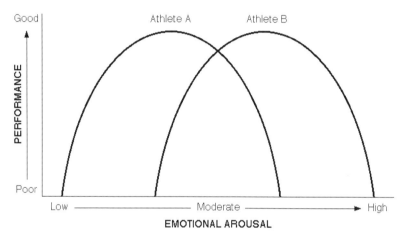

One way to block out the influence of spectators and to manage anxiety at optimum levels is to apply the concentration, relaxation, cognitive and behavioural skills described in Part Two of this book in order to focus on the game, point by point, whilst blocking out all external distractions, including people who might be watching, as well as our unhelpful internal distractions such as over-breathing, muscle tension and negative automatic thoughts. Part Two of this book will describe anxiety management techniques in detail, including the somatic techniques of deep breathing and progressive relaxation, the cognitive techniques of distraction, thought stopping, positive self-talk and visualisation, and the behavioural strategies of preparation, coping with gamesmanship and positive body language.

PART TWO

MANAGING ANXIETY

SOMATIC TECHNIQUES

CHAPTER THREE
Breathing

Chapter Objectives

After reading this chapter you will be able to describe:

The differences between deep & shallow breathing

The benefits of deep breathing

After reading this chapter you will know how to:

Do deep breathing exercises

David rushes to the net from the baseline to chase down a drop shot. He just makes it before the ball hits the ground for the second time. The pain in his lungs seems nothing compared to his sense of achievement. His pride lasts but a nanosecond as his return lacks control and falls straight at the feet of his opponent who hits a top spin lob over his head to the back of the court.

David briefly considers conceding the point, but he is known for his 'never say die' attitude and instead decides to chase down the lob. He sprints to the back of the court, swipes at the ball and runs headfirst into the wire fence. He looks up only to see his opponent at the net smash the ball into court for the point.

David is proud of his effort but stands bent over, hands on his knees, head down. He can feel his lungs about to burst. He takes in a deep breath, then another and another. Nothing. His chest feels tighter and tighter. He starts to feel dizzy. He breathes faster and faster in an attempt to get some much needed oxygen into his body. He can almost hear his heart beating like a drum. He wishes he had let his opponent win the point. Now he is so tired and feels so light headed that when he comes to serve for the next point he can barely toss the ball never mind hit it over the net. Fault. Double fault. Game lost.

Deep breathing

We breathe on average 20,000 times every day. Although breathing is natural, something we do without thinking, awake or asleep, a great many people breathe incorrectly. In fact, when asked to take a deep breath, most people do the exact opposite and take a very shallow breath. Typically, whilst trying to take a deep breath, they raise their shoulders and suck in their stomachs. Essentially, this only uses the top part of the lungs.

Often, people find that they are breathing too fast, which can actually lead to a condition called 'hyperventilation' or 'over breathing'. Hyperventilation is rapid or deep breathing, usually caused by anxiety, in which fast, shallow breathes through the mouth cause us to take in too much oxygen whilst blowing out carbon dioxide too quickly, affecting health.

When blood vessels contain too much oxygen and just small traces of carbon dioxide, the oxygen cannot get into the body's tissues and instead clings to the blood. Shallow breathing does not give the muscles and brain the amount of oxygen needed to function correctly. Shallow breathing can create muscular tension, tiredness, interfere with athletic activity and produce aches, pains and illness.

The average rate of breathing for adults is 12-20 breaths

per minute at rest, although 'average' does not necessarily equate to good or healthy and reducing breaths per minute to 10 or fewer is probably the optimum rate of breathing for a healthy person at rest. Some scientists consider that in training, about 15 or so breathes per minute is the right level to maintain good oxygen flow. Although we may at times try and breathe faster and faster in order to take in more oxygen when tired, this will serve only to have the opposite effect and produce hyperventilation and fatigue.

Learning to breathe deeply initiates the activity of the para-sympathetic nervous system and elicits the relaxation response, reducing stress and impacting positively on general health.

Deep breathing can relieve all types of aches and pains, from headaches to backache, from stomachaches to chest pains. Deep breathing allows the blood pressure to return to a normal level; it releases the body's natural 'feel good' hormones (endorphins).

Learning how to breathe correctly has in certain studies been linked to lowered blood pressure, reduced symptoms of depression, fewer hot flushes in menopausal women, increased fertility and even a reduction in cancerous cells.

Benefits of Deep Breathing

Slows heart rate

Reduces arousal

Relaxes muscles

Refocuses attention

Reduces anxiety

Diverts attention

Offers a sense of control

Are you a shallow or deep breather?

There is an easy exercise to do to identify whether you are a shallow or deep breather. Place your left hand against your lower abdomen and your right hand on your chest. Breathe out completely. Now take a deep breath. If the hand on your stomach moves out when you breathe in and the air seems to flow in easily to the bottom of your stomach, you are breathing deeply. If when you take a breath, the hand on your stomach moves in as your stomach pulls in, and the hand on your chest moves out as your diaphragm expands, you are breathing too shallowly.

Breathing exercises

Deep breathing is the simplest and most basic method of relaxation. Often, the first sign from our body that we are becoming stressed is when we start to breathe rapidly with shallow breaths. This can often then lead to increased palpitations.

Taking deep, slow breaths reduces the heart rate, slowing it down and therefore reducing physiological arousal. Deep breathing helps relax the muscles in the shoulder and neck. It can provide an opportunity to focus attention away from the stress of the game. Deep, slow breathing can be an immediate, accessible and powerful way of reducing physical anxiety on-court during a match. It is also very helpful to utilise this at the break between games.

One of the best things about breathing exercises is that they are quick and easy to do; they can be done at any time and in any place without drawing the attention of others to what you are doing. Follow the following instructions:

1. Breathe out deeply, contracting the abdomen.

2. Breathe in slowly as you expand the abdomen.

3. Continue to breathe as you expand the chest.

4. Continue to breathe in as you raise up your shoulders towards your ears.

5. Hold the breath for a count of 3.

6. Breathe out slowly for a count of 6.

7. Relax the muscles of your shoulders and chest completely.

8. Repeat 3 or 4-times until there is a sensation of calmness.

9. At the same time, it is helpful to focus on positive self-talk (see chapter 6).

CHAPTER FOUR
Relaxation

Chapter Objectives

After reading this chapter you will be able to describe:

What relaxation is

The benefits of relaxation

The stages of progressive relaxation

After reading this chapter you will know how to:

Relax deeply and quickly

Relaxation is a psychological treatment procedure to deal with the sensory components of anxiety and stress, particularly feelings of muscular tightness and pressure. It is designed to reduce the build-up of stress and to short-circuit physiological arousal. Relaxation has been shown to have predictable, reproducible physiological changes, including decreased oxygen consumption and carbon-dioxide elimination; reductions in heart rate, respiration and arterial blood lactate; increased skeletal muscle blood flow; and increased slow alpha wave intensity on electroencephalogram (EEG) studies. All of these changes are consistent with decreased activity of the autonomic nervous system and hence relaxation of the body.

Even if increased muscle tension is regarded as a consequence rather than a cause of stress, eliciting the relaxation response at the onset of tension may circumvent any sympathetic arousal which may have otherwise exacerbated the tension.

In addition, engaging in relaxation exercises may legitimise the temporary avoidance of certain stressors, allowing the person to become relaxed despite those stressors and thereby deal more effectively with them. Relaxation may divert attention from stress and tension, allowing a sense of immediate control and coping.

Relaxation is a skill to be learned and mastered with practice. Learning to relax the muscles in one's body takes time and will involve a certain amount of practice off-court. Progressive relaxation is a particularly effective technique for reducing bodily tension, as with practice the individual can learn the difference between a tense and a relaxed state—which are mutually exclusive in that it is simply not possible to be both relaxed and tense at the same time. With practice, the technique can be applied to specific areas—for example, in tennis, the muscles of the arm or shoulder.

At the outset, relaxation probably requires 20—30-minutes of concentrated effort; over time, it should be possible to relax the entire body within a couple of seconds. Investing in practice off-court will pay dividends on-court—try it for a few weeks and see how much more relaxed you become in your game.

Benefits of Relaxation

Reduces the build up of stress

Short-circuits arousal

Reduces muscle tension

Reduces heart rate

Slows down breathing

Decreases oxygen consumption

Decreases carbon-dioxide elimination

Increases blood flow

Diverts attention

Offers a sense of control

Progressive Relaxation

Progressive relaxation was pioneered in the 1930's by physiologist and psychologist Edmund Jacobson. He believed that if people could learn to relax their muscles in a precise, progressive method, then psychological or mental relaxation would follow. He developed a technique in which various voluntary muscle groups throughout the body were tensed and relaxed in an orderly sequence.

There is a range of relaxation techniques available, although perhaps the most popular is that developed by Ost. He described a stage model of relaxation, in the first stage of which the body is divided up into a series of large muscle groups and each group is tensed and then relaxed in turn. By alternating tension and relaxation, one can learn to discriminate between these two states and to become more aware of any parts of the body that are particularly tense.

Once the basic technique is learned, shorter forms are

taught in which fewer groups of muscles are relaxed; and finally in which relaxation occurs whilst engaged in everyday activities—including tennis.

The initial relaxation stage

In the initial stages of relaxation, 16-groups of muscles are progressively tensed and relaxed. These are: the right hand and forearm, right upper arm, left hand and forearm, left upper arm, forehead, eyes and cheeks, mouth and jaw, shoulders and neck, chest and back, abdomen, right thigh, right calf, right foot, left thigh, left calf and left foot.

The intermediate relaxation stage

In the intermediate stage of relaxation training, the 16 muscle groups are reduced to 8 muscle groups by focusing on the right and left arm, the eyes and mouth, the neck, the shoulders and chest, the stomach and both legs.

The advanced relaxation stage

In advanced relaxation, the 8-muscle groups are combined concurrently and all muscle groups are tensed at the same time before releasing all tension in one big wave.

Passive relaxation

There are also more passive means of relaxation that involve concentrating on the body followed by imagining a sense of heaviness in the particular muscle group.

The Relaxation Stages

STAGE	NUMBER OF MUSCLE GROUPS
Initial	16
Intermediate	8
Advanced	All at once
Passive	In imagination only

Instructions for the initial relaxation stage (16 muscle groups)

Sit comfortably in a chair with support for your head, or lie on your bed. Close you eyes and concentrate on your breathing. Allow your breathing to become deep, slow and even. Imagine that with every breath you take the whole of your body is becoming more and more deeply relaxed. Spend a minute or two focusing on breathing in this way. Once you have achieved a focused and relaxed state of breathing, undertake the following instructions:

Hand and lower arms imagine holding a tennis ball in your right hand. Squeeze it hard. Feel the tightness in your hand and arm as you squeeze. Now drop the tennis ball. Notice how your muscles feel when they are relaxed. (Repeat for left hand and arm).

Upper arms bend your right arm so that your hand comes up towards your shoulder. Pretend that in the bend of your arm you have a walnut, which you are trying to crack. Make your arm really tense to crack that nut. Now relax and let your hand go back to your side. Notice how your muscles feel now they are relaxed. (Repeat for the left arm).

Forehead   imagine that a fly has landed on your forehead. You cannot use your hands to get rid of it; try to wriggle your forehead, frown and make a face with the top part of your head to get that fly away. Now relax, the fly has gone. Notice all the tight and tense feelings go away from your forehead as the muscles become more and more relaxed.

Eyes and cheeks   wait a minute, that fly is back! This time he has landed on your nose. Wrinkle up your nose and eyes to try to get him to fly away. He has flown away now so you can relax your face. Notice that when you screwed up your nose and eyes and then relaxed, your whole body relaxed too. Notice how good that feels.

Mouth and jaw   imagine that you have a giant bubble gum in your mouth. It is very hard to chew, but bite down on it hard and try to chew. Now relax and just let your jaw hang loose. Notice the muscles relax as you stop chewing.

Shoulders and neck   put your hands behind your head and push back as if you are about to let out a big stretch and yawn. Feel the muscles in your shoulder pull as you stretch higher. Now relax. Notice all the tension drain away from the muscles in your shoulders and neck. Notice how good that feels.

Chest and back

this time I want you to take a great deep breath as though you are about to blow out 100 candles on a birthday cake; but hold the breath, do not let it out. Now let it out slowly. As you let out the breath, notice how the muscles in your chest and your back relax. Try and get your breathing back to a nice, slow, steady rate again.

Abdomen

imagine that you are lying on the floor and a cat is about to come over and walk on your stomach. He will not hurt you, but you do need to make your stomach tense and hard. Tighten up those stomach muscles and hold them for a few seconds. He has gone now, you can relax. Notice the difference between how the muscles in your stomach felt when they were tight and then relaxed.

Thighs

push your right foot down hard onto the floor as though you are trying to push it through the floorboards. Now let it relax and notice all the tightness drain away from the muscles that are completely relaxed. (Repeat for left thigh).

Calves

lift up your right foot slightly and bring your toes towards you, as though you are trying to touch your knee with your toes. Notice the tightness in the muscles at the back of your calf. Relax and put your foot gently down to the floor. Notice the tightness drain away. (Repeat for left calf).

Feet

I want you to pretend that you are standing in your bare feet in a paddling pool filled with mud. Squish your toes down deeply into the mud and try to get your foot through the mud to the bottom of the paddling pool. Move your toes about and feel the mud squish up between them. Now relax your foot and let your toes go loose and notice how good it feels to be relaxed. (Repeat with left foot).

Ending

now that you have done all the exercises, for a few minutes or so try to stay relaxed, calm and comfortable in your chair or whilst lying on the bed. Try to notice the feeling of relaxation in the muscles all over your body. Now, imagine that you are in a safe, comfortable relaxing place—perhaps at the beach, in the countryside or a favourite holiday destination. In you mind's eye, draw upon all of your senses to relive the relaxing experiences. After a minute or so, open your eyes, stretch or yawn. For the remainder of the day, try to remember how good it felt to be relaxed.

Practice these exercises every day; let the skill of relaxation help you become more and more relaxed and in turn improve your game.

Instructions for the intermediate relaxation stage

1.**Arms** Hold both arms out, slightly bent at the elbow. Tense the hands, lower arms and upper arms. Relax.

2.**Chest and breathing** Take a deep breath and hold it for a few seconds before slowing releasing.

3.**Neck** Slightly hunch your shoulders whilst drawing the neck in and back.

4.**Face** Close your eyes tightly and draw in the rest of your face muscles.

Instructions for the advanced relaxation stage

Take a deep, slow breath. Sit forward in the chair and tense all muscle groups at the same time before releasing all the tension in one big wave. Repeat this 4 times, followed by a suggestion of heaviness, a couple of minutes of relaxation and a stretch at the end.

Instructions for passive relaxation

To become relaxed without going through the relaxation cycle, recall what the relaxed state felt like in your mind and try to achieve that state without tensing the muscles. Focus your attention on the muscles and carefully identify any feeling or sensations of tension or tightness; especially focus on any tension feelings. Then relax and recall what it is like to become more and more deeply relaxed. This exercise can be undertaken with specific muscle groups:

1. Both arms.

2. Both legs.

3. Abdomen.

4. Chest.

5. Shoulders.

6. Neck.

7. Face.

Tips for relaxing more deeply

1. Do your exercises in loose fitting, comfortable clothing.

2. Do your exercises in a comfortable chair, with support for your neck and head, or lying on your bed.

3. Do your exercises in a darkened room—if it is light outside, draw the curtains.

4. Do your exercises in a quiet room. We cannot completely avoid noisy distractions but switch off the television or stereo and ask your family or friends not to disturb you for a while.

5. Do your exercises at least twice per day. Continued better practice will increase the ease with which you can relax more quickly and deeply.

6. Make each session last at least 20-minutes. Practice using a clock to time yourself against.

7. Begin your exercises by concentrating on your breathing—develop a slow, steady rate. Think about becoming more and more relaxed with every breath you take.

8. Once your breathing is steady, go through the sequence of exercises you have learned.

9. Finish your exercises by concentrating on a deep state of relaxation. Remember how good that feels.

10. Remember—practice makes perfect!

COGNITIVE
TECHNIQUES

CHAPTER FIVE
Distraction

Chapter Objectives

After reading this chapter you will be able to describe:

Why distraction is helpful

Name several distraction techniques

After reading this chapter you will know how to:

Focus on an object

Use sensory awareness

Draw upon positive memories

Stop unwanted thoughts

Postpone your worries

Simply trying not to think about something once the thought has entered your mind can be very difficult indeed—right now, try not to think about a giraffe. What did you think about? A giraffe, of course!

Have you ever noticed that once you become aware of something the very act of noticing can make things seem worse? This is very true of physical symptoms of anxiety—as soon as you notice them, the symptoms worsen. For example, noticing that you are short of breath makes it harder to breathe, at least at first.

Distraction techniques intervene in the vicious cycle of

anxiety. They offer immediate management of symptoms and are a very helpful way of providing evidence that one has some control over feelings of anxiety. They provide an immediate sense of control and are particularly useful in situations where it is difficult to challenge negative automatic thoughts.

There are several different types of distraction techniques, including focusing on an object, sensory awareness, positive memories, thought stopping and postponement.

Focusing on an object

Most distraction techniques require one to focus on external factors. Try to focus right now on the sensation of your right foot inside your shoe. Now shift your attention to the feeling of your tongue inside your mouth. Concentrate on your tongue. Can you still feel your foot inside your shoe at the same time? Almost certainly not because the focus of your concentration had shifted.

Because it is difficult to truly focus one's attention on more than one thing at a time, in situations where negative thoughts, self-doubt and a heightened awareness of physiological arousal are interfering with your ability to play, focusing on a single object in as much detail as possible can help refocus your attention away from the stressful situation.

Focusing on an object on the tennis court at times of intense or heightened anxiety or stress offers an immediate distraction and a consequent reduction in feelings of arousal and tension. Between points or at change rounds you can focus on anything you choose—your shoe, sweatband, drink or racquet. For example, during the break between games, you could look at your tennis shoe and focus on its size, shape, colour, the stitching or logo.

During the point, you will need to be focused on the

movement of the ball. Brad Gilbert has described how he sometimes focuses upon the writing on the tennis ball, trying to read the maker's name as the ball approaches, suggesting that with practice, like any skill, the ability to do so develops.

Sensory awareness

A related technique is to focus on one of your senses—sight, sound, vision, taste or touch. Often the easiest to access is the sense of touch, perhaps feeling the pressure of the sweatband on your wrist; or the grip of your hand on the tennis racquet; or the connection between your trainer sole and the ground as you prepare to serve—therein allowing immediate distraction from the feelings of anxiety which inhibit performance.

With practice, sensory awareness can involve focusing on one's entire surroundings. Look around the court and ask yourself what you can see, hear, feel. Can you feel the racquet in your hand? Can you hear the thud of the ball? Can you feel the sun and wind on your face? Can you smell the sweat in the air?

Positive memories

Another technique is that of trying to recall a concrete and vivid pleasant memory in order to provide a helpful distraction and instil a feeling of relaxation and calmness. Try vividly recalling the memory of a good serve as you are about to serve. This is a variation of the visualisation technique which can distract you from feelings of anxiety, decreasing muscular tension in the shoulder and arm, resulting in a better technique, a faster, more accurate serve and the reduced likelihood of serving a fault.

Thought stopping

Under pressure, it is perfectly normal to have negative thoughts, laden by self-doubt. For example, how often have you known in your heart that you are going to double-fault on your second serve? I'm sure this has happened to all of us. How often have you known that even though you were 5-2 up and serving for the game, you would not be able to hold your serve and your opponent would get back into the match and even beat you?

These are examples of so called 'self-fulfilling prophecies'—variation of negative self-talk that produces muscular tension and inhibits coordination and produces mistakes. Self-fulfilling prophecies can cause the player to focus so much on what *not* to do that they somehow almost forget what they have to do—for example, they become so focused on avoiding double-faulting that they lose all sense of where they should serve. This kind of difficulty is not unique to tennis; it is common to all individual sports.

Negative automatic thoughts are 'negative' because they are linked with unpleasant feelings and 'automatic' because they enter your head quickly, without being invited or pondered or reasoned through. As you become increasingly anxious, the negative automatic thoughts become more frequent and more negative and can then dominate thinking, destroy confidence and damage performance.

Sometimes, such negative thoughts can become repetitive and play on our minds so that they are difficult to shake-off; they set up predictable patterns of behaviour including 'choking' in crunch situations. The more this happens, the more anxious we become and the more likely we are to make mistakes—this is the vicious cycle of negative thoughts, anxious feelings and behavioural mistakes.

One way of preventing negative automatic thoughts dominating our way of thinking is to use a cognitive-behavioural technique known as 'thought stopping.' Thought stopping is a simple behavioural technique to help eliminate various repetitive negative thoughts. Thought stopping is the process of consciously and deliberately changing ways of thinking in order to break destructive patterns of behaviour. It is a psychological technique to reduce the negative impact of stress.

Quite simply, thought stopping involves replacing one thought for another—that is, replacing a negative thought with a positive thought. This helps clear the mind of dysfunctional thoughts which increase stress, whilst introducing positive thoughts that aid relaxation and coping.

Try the following method—**STOP!, SWAP, BREATHE, REPEAT.**

STOP!	when you experience an anxiety provoking thought, say to yourself firmly, 'Stop!' Say this loudly inside your head if to actually say it out loud would cause you too much embarrassment.
SWAP	Immediately replace the negative thought with a positive statement such as, 'I can…' or 'I will…'
BREATHE	Take a deep breath using the techniques described earlier in this book. This is important because it will allow you to associate relaxation with positive thinking.
REPEAT	Do steps 1 through to 3 every time you have a negative automatic thought. With practice, this will become automatic and negative thoughts will reduce and hopefully eliminate themselves.

Postponement

If you find that leading up to a match you are pre-occupied with worrying thoughts, then one way to reduce their impact is to give yourself permission to postpone your worries until a later time. For example, instead of constantly thinking about and worrying over your match two hours before you are due to play, why not give yourself permission to think about it just 30-minutes before the game?—which will simply mean that you have 1 ½ hours less worry time.

Distraction Techniques

Focusing on an Object

Sensory Awareness

Positive Memories

Thought Stopping

Postponement

STOP!, SWAP, BREATHE, REPEAT

CHAPTER SIX
Self-talk

Chapter Objectives

After reading this chapter you will be able to:
Define self-talk
Give examples of positive and negative self-talk

After reading this chapter you will know how to:
Use positive self-talk
Challenge negative automatic thoughts
Self-monitor
Conduct a behavioural experiment

'Self-talk' is language that is directed inwardly to the self. It includes thoughts, personal statements or words said aloud or privately inside one's head. Self-talk can be 'positive' or 'negative' and either helpful or a hindrance to your game.

Negative self-talk

Negative self-talk is critical and increases anxiety. Saying negative things to one's self such as, 'that was rubbish' or 'I am never going to win this game', simply leaves you feeling bad about yourself. Negative self-talk increases muscle tension and somatic arousal; it leads to feelings of anxiety or anger; it can distil a deep sense of despair or hopelessness. Negative self-talk causes de-motivation and makes you less rather than more likely to improve performance and win the game.

Positive self-talk

In contrast, positive self-talk, such as simple phrases like, 'I can do it!' or 'keep going!', helps increase effort, energy and builds a positive mental attitude. Positive self-talk maintains emotional stability, keeps you calm, more focused, optimistic and energised—and therefore more likely to improve your performance and win the game.

Self-talk and performance

Research has shown that in sport in general, including tennis in particular, negative self-talk is associated with losing; players who report believing in the usefulness of positive self-talk win more points than players who do not believe in self-talk—suggesting that the type of self-talk engaged in by tennis players influences the outcome of competition.

Excuses

Don't make excuses before you play. Excuses are just mental preparation for losing. How often have you heard people say before a game such things as that they were up late last night, didn't sleep, have a hangover, a 'dodgy' knee, sore back or a headache? In reality, even if these things are true, they are just variations of negative self-talk spoken out loud to your opponent. They will only serve to lower your self-belief and increase the self-confidence of your opponent. If you really are not fit to play—then don't play. Cancel or rearrange the match.

The table below shows the positive and negative effects of self-talk.

Self-Talk

POSITIVE	NEGATIVE
Keeps Calm	Increases Anxiety
Maintains Emotional Stability	Arouses Anger
Increases Energy	Bad Feelings about Self
Increases Effort	Despair
Stays Focussed	Hopelessness
Optimism	De-motivation
Improved Performance	Under Performance

Self-monitoring

Of course, many people are unaware of their negative thinking—it has become so established that it is perfectly normal to them. Their negative thoughts are very much automatic. Indeed, with some people, a positive thought about themselves is like a swallow in winter—not seen very often.

In order to become more self-aware, it might be necessary for some people to keep a diary as a way of self-monitoring their negative thoughts. This can be most helpful in identifying the situations in which the negative thoughts occur, the exact nature of the thoughts and how they make you feel.

Recording doesn't have to be overly complicated or time-consuming. It is perfectly acceptable to make simple, brief entries in a small notebook. Keep this notebook in your racquet bag so that you can make the entries as close as possible in time to the actual event—often leaving too long a gap can produce distorted recordings, not least because the feeling or affective state associated with the thought has long gone.

Below is an example of the kind of record you might like to design for yourself.

A Record of Negative Thoughts & Feelings

What Happened	Thoughts	Feeling
Missed an 'easy' volley Serving to stay in the set Double faulted Lost match	'I am a fool.' 'I must not miss.' 'I am rubbish.' 'I am not good enough to play in this league. I am withdrawing.'	Anger Anxiety Shame Despair

If you practice working on this often enough, it will eventually become comfortable and almost automatic—that is, negative automatic thoughts will be replaced by positive automatic thoughts. Below is an example of how positive automatic thoughts this might look in recorded form.

A Record of Positive Thoughts & Feelings

What Happened	Thoughts	Feeling
Missed an 'easy' volley Serving to stay in the set Double faulted Lost match	'I was in the right position for that shot.' 'I can do it!.' 'Keep going! Stay positive!' 'I played well. What can I learn from this match to take into my next match?'	Increased effort Staying focussed Emotional stability Optimism

Tips for replacing negative with positive self-talk

Under conditions of stress, we tend to fall back upon old, deeply engrained ways of thinking and behaving. Old habits die hard. If old habits are unhelpful, then they are bad habits that we need to change. It is much easier to practice changing the way we think and behave—including learning how to replace negative self-talk with positive self-talk—in conditions of reduced or less stress. So, begin learning to change how you think off-court, in practice sessions or 'knocks' with friends, before transferring your skills, little by little, into competitive situations in which the challenge to be different will be much more difficult.

Much self-talk for a tense or anxious player is likely to be negative. Practice changing negative statements to positive ones—change 'I can't' to 'I can' statements. It is important to interrupt negative self-talk as soon as it occurs and then immediately change it into positive self-talk. One of the first steps to improving your self-talk is to make a list of your thoughts immediately following a match. These can be written down in a diary at courtside using the exact words or phrases you used during the game.

Following this, the next step is to eliminate all negative thoughts by stopping them before they interfere with performance. The second you become aware of the negative thoughts, refocus, shift concentration and take a deep breath. Then learn to replace the negative thought with a positive self-statement.

Although it is likely that you will become self-conscious—perhaps even feel silly at times—in changing the way you think about yourself, shifting from negative to positive self-talk is a vital ingredient of becoming a winner—the less negative you are, the more likely you are to win.

In general, self-talk has been found to be most helpful when it is:

SHORT

keep self-talk to single words such as 'Go!' or short phrases such as, 'Come on!' or 'Keep going!'

SPECIFIC

use instructional statements such as, 'Keep your eyes on the ball' or 'Don't forget to split-step', rather than vague statements such as, 'Play better' or 'Try harder.'

PERSONAL

make statements personal, begin them with 'I…', which will increase your sense of self-control and self-efficacy.

PRESENT

focus on the present. Forget the past. Forget your last shot. Forget the score. Focus on one point at a time—the current point that is occurring in the 'here and now'. Instead of thinking, 'That was rubbish, how did I miss such an easy shot?' say to yourself something like, 'Concentrate on the next point and make sure I return the serve in play'.

POSITIVE

frame your self-talk using positive words such as 'Yes!', 'Be strong!', 'Do it!' Rather than saying, 'I don't miss down the line' say 'I hit winners down the line'. Change negative labels such as 'stupid' to positive ones such as 'I can do it'

SOLUTION FOCUSED

focus on solutions instead of problems. Change words such as 'should', 'ought', 'have to', 'must' to words such as 'could', 'can', 'will'. Don't think about what you 'mustn't' or 'shouldn't do'; think instead about what you should or can do. For example, instead of thinking, 'I must not double-fault now or I will lose the game' change this to 'I'll make sure that my first serve goes in'.

REALISTIC

don't over dramatise or catastrophize—avoid expecting the worst and instead expect a more positive outcome. Avoid over-generalising, for example losing a single point, a game, a set or even the first two sets in a best-of-five match does not necessarily mean you will lose the next point, game, set or match.

How to use Self-Talk

Short—use single words
Specific—instructional terms
Personal—begin with 'I…'
Present—in the 'here and now'
Solution focussed—what can do
Realistic—keep grounded

BE POSITIVE!

Challenging negative automatic thoughts

Psychologists have developed many ways of challenging negative automatic thoughts. Try some of these basic methods. See which ones are most relevant to your specific situation and which ones are helpful to your unique cognitive style:

EVIDENCE   what supporting evidence do I have to show that this thought is true?

For example, do I always lose? Do I always double fault at break points? Do I always miss when I come to the net?

ALTERNATIVES   is there any other way of looking at the situation? Is there any evidence to argue against a negative automatic thought? Are there any exceptions to the rules?

For example, did I miss that volley but was in the right position at the net? Did I double fault but only for the second time in the set? Did I miss that top-spin backhand down the line but kept the rally going with my top-spin backhand cross court? Did I lose this match but win the previous match?

OTHERS   What would other people say about me? What would other people say my strengths are?

For example, I am quite sure that you could happily list your faults and weaknesses, but why not make a list of your strengths and ask others (your playing partners or your coach) to make a list of what they consider to be the strengths of your game.

REALISTIC   Am I being realistic or unrealistic? Am I setting myself unobtainable standards? Are my expectations too high?

For example, did I lose because I was playing badly or because my opponent was actually a better player than I am? Did I miss that serve at a crucial point in the match by trying to hit it too hard and too close to the centre line when I probably should have just served with medium pace and depth at this stage of the game?

LEARNING   How steep is my learning curve? Separate the wood from the trees— how were you playing a year ago? 6 month ago? If your learning curve is very steep, how were you playing a few weeks ago? How do you think you will be playing in 6 weeks time? Six months time?

CHALLENGE   Challenge your negative automatic thoughts with rational coping statements. For example, if you miss a shot, say to yourself 'Everyone makes mistakes.'

Ask yourself if you are selecting out one or two examples of poor play and ignoring all the good shots? For example, if after the game you find yourself focusing only on the double-faults you served, work out exactly how many serves you did in the entire match and what percentage of them were double-faults compared to successful serves. You can do a similar thing with all of your shots—backhands, forehands, volleys, lobs and smashes.

Self-monitoring—a behavioural experiment

Many players, at all levels, argue that they 'need' their anxious and angry feelings and their negative self-talk to motivate themselves to do well, particularly to change the course of a match if they are losing. People often argue that if they stopped swearing or criticising themselves verbally on court, their game would deteriorate further and they would simply lose. A standard argument one hears up and down the land is that 'it never did John McEnroe's game any harm'.

Well, of course that is not something we can easily quantify, although McEnroe himself has since acknowledged that his temper probably cost him more games than it won him over the course of his career. Of course, we are all unique individuals and everybody has different learning styles and ways of motivating themselves. However, for every successful John McEnroe there are many thousands for whom behaving in an angry or aggressive manner on court is detrimental to their game.

Don't take my word for it. Try a simple behavioural experiment—be your own psychologist. It is probably easier to get somebody else to do this for you but it is possible to do it yourself if you are able to accurately self-monitor. Simply record every instance of negative self-talk or body language during a match. Then record whether or not you won or lost the point immediately following the negative talk or behaviour.

At the end of the match you will have a simple two-column outcome—points won and points lost following negative talk and behaviour. See which column is the longest to determine whether such behaviour has been helpful or a hindrance to your game. If you are really good at self-monitoring, you could do a similar thing to include points won or lost after internalised negative self-talk.

Behavioural Experiment

Negative Self-Talk	Points (tick if won)
☐ ☐ ☐ ☐	☐ ☐ ☐ ☐

Tips for self-monitoring

SIMPLE   Self-monitoring is best kept simple—if you make it too complicated, it will be difficult to analyse your findings. Over-complication can also make you less motivated to actually self-monitor in the first place.

IMMEDIATE   Self-monitoring should be done immediately and recorded in written form as
soon as possible after the event. This
will increase its reliability and accuracy.

RECORDED   One of the easiest ways to do this is to
have an easily accessible notepad and
pen in your bag at the side of the court
so that you can make notes during the
game. A structured form or recording
device will assist this process.

Remember however that self-monitoring produces something known by psychologists as 'reactivity'—that is, when
you notice and record something, its frequency will often
change as you become more self-aware of what you are doing, which then may cause you to alter your behaviour. For
example, if you start to record every instance of on-court
negative self-talk you will become aware of what you are
doing and may therefore make fewer self-critical statements
in response.

CHAPTER SEVEN
Visualisation

Chapter Objectives

After reading this chapter you will be able to describe:

What visualisation is

The benefits of visualisation

After reading this chapter you will know how to:

Visualise successfully

Visualisation, also referred to at times as mental imagery, guided imagery, mental rehearsal or meditation, refers to the creation or re-creation of an experience in the mind. Visualisation involves drawing upon the memory of a previous event in order to practice mentally events that have yet to occur. Visualisation is a major tool of sport psychology; it is a form of mental practice or rehearsal of shots in one's mind before they are tried out physically—for example, the serve you are going to make, the return you are about to hit, past matches from which you want to replay errors or even future matches you want to win.

Visualisation can be internal or 'associated', in which we picture a shot that we are hitting; or it can be external or 'disassociated', in which it is as though we are outside of ourselves, watching like a spectator as we play a shot. Visualisation can also be used to re-create emotional states such as anxiety, anger or happiness. Just like actual physical practice and drills, visualisation has an impact upon the nervous system and muscles of the body, making connections that allow certain shots to be performed and therefore helping us to react in certain situations without having to consciously think about them all of the time. Visualisation also reduces anxiety, focuses concentration, improves confidence—by making you believe that you can make a shot—and helps with creative problem solving.

Scientific research evidence shows that visualisation can enhance performance in a whole range of sports and sports psychologists have found that the use of visualisation differentiates between elite and non-elite, successful and less successful athletes.

Benefits of Visualisation

Reduces anxiety

Focuses concentration

Improves belief

Boosts confidence

Improves problem solving

Makes connection in the nervous system

Speeds up reaction times

Enhances Performance

Tips for successful visualisation

Visualisation is a skill to be acquired through repetition and practice and therefore like any skill it is best built-up by including it as part of one's general training sessions and during breaks in matches, sometimes referred to as 'dead time'.

Because it is easier to practice new skills in a more relaxed state, away from the arousal and demands of competition, it is best to practice visualisation skills away from the tennis court and in a quiet location before trying to transfer your skills to the on-court situation and a match.

Successful visualisation draws upon all of the senses. Particularly in the case of tennis, visualisation focuses on the kinaesthetic (movement) sense, important because it involves the use of muscles and joints—necessary for all sporting activity. Images can also be visual (for example, the serve hitting the line) or auditory (for example, the thud of a smash).

On court, one of the most appropriate and helpful ways to use visualisation is before a serve or before a return of serve, when the waiting time is longer than it is during a rally. You can visualise your swing, the bounce of the ball or where you plan to hit the serve in your opponent's half of the court. You can also visualise your movement into the court following the serve as well as your winning volley at the net.

You can visualise your good shots as well as the shots you need to improve. Visualisation of improving shots is a particularly helpful skill to utilise in slow motion. You can visualise with or without a racquet in your hand, with or without an actual swing. If you watch the professionals, you will often see them playing an 'air shot' when they have made a mistake on court as a way of playing the shot again in their mind, this time hitting the ball correctly and improving coordination and confidence for the next time they have to make the same or a similar shot.

It is helpful to visualise successful scenarios where we win points and matches in order to follow game plans that work well; but also at times to imagine scenarios where the game plan is not working and we are losing, in order to help us imagine changing our plan if needed.

The PETTLEP model

Holmes and Collins have developed the PETTLEP model which they suggest should be followed in order to use visualisation effectively.

PHYSICAL sometimes relaxation and at other times heightening arousal is helpful prior to practising visualisation. Use deep breathing or relaxation techniques if you need to be relaxed in order to visualise a newly learnt shot. Play a few shots and run around the court if you need to get your blood and adrenaline pumping, for example in order to re-access the heightened physical and emotional state of an actual match.

ENVIRONMENT use multi-sensory cues specific to the environment you want to imagine or visualise, for example by looking at photographs or video tapes of your game or your opponent's matches.

TASK consider the exact nature of the task and whether this requires you to practice an external image or to practice making decisions. For example, do you need to visualise a top spin backhand or should you be visualising whether to hit the shot cross court or down the line?

TIMING

once you have a sense of mastery, imagine playing in real time rather than slowing or speeding up actual time.   .

LEARNING

the image can change as learning takes place. You can make it more complicated or add more components to the image.

EMOTION

try and include an emotional element to the imagery so that it has greater meaning for you. For example, try and access the feeling when you hit an ace or made a passing shot down the line.

PERSPECTIVE

consider both internal and external images. Sometimes visualise the shot and see the ball fly; sometimes visualise yourself as though you were watching from above or from the side.

Below are two practice mental imagery scenarios for you to have a go at visualisation. Try them and see how they feel for you. Try them several times until they feel comfortable and you have some success at accessing the imagery in your mind's eye. Then, when you feel ready, try your own visualisation, making it unique to your own style of play.

Writing it down first can help. Edit it if necessary to make it fit your unique and individual needs. As you get better at visualisation and the imagery becomes easier, change and adapt your scripts and draw up a range of scenarios to make full advantage of your newly acquired psychological skills.

Practice visualisation 1: preparation for the match

Close your eyes. Take slow, deep breaths. Imagine yourself becoming more and more deeply relaxed with every breath you take. Allow the sensation of relaxation to wash over your entire body. When you are deeply relaxed you are ready to begin the visualisation.

Imagine arriving on court. Notice everything around you. Draw upon all of your senses. See the colour of the playing surface. Visualise the seats around the court, the net, the umpire's chair. Hear the sounds of other people warming up around you, the thud of tennis balls. Feel the air on your face. Smell the atmosphere. Notice how you feel inside your body—a tingly, excited sensation as your body prepares for the match.

Now imagine yourself warming-up. See yourself stretching gently, loosening up, jogging, moving slowly and steadily about the court as you warm up your muscles in preparation for the game.

Now imagine taking your racquet from your bag. Imagine the feel of the racquet in your hand, its weight and balance. Visualise a few practice shots, feeling the movements of your arm, legs and body in a relaxed way.

Imagine hitting the ball and the ball going exactly where you want it to go in your opponent's half. Visualise forehands, backhands, top spin and slice, all hit with depth, accuracy and as much power and control as you need. Then visualise coming into the net to hit deep volleys and 'slam-dunk' smashes, effortlessly and with relaxed ease.

Now imagine yourself talking positively and making positive self-statements such as, 'I am playing really well...I feel strong...I can hit my serve exactly where I want....I am a winner.'

Now imagine the match beginning. Visualise your serve as you bounce the ball, take a breath, toss the ball up high, swing, connect with the ball and hit it exactly where you aimed. An outright ace.

Now imagine a short rally as you move freely about the court, on your toes all of the time, breathing easily and steadily as the ball goes exactly where you aimed, every time. You are completely in control.

Practice visualisation 2: the serve

Close your eyes. Take slow, deep breaths. Imagine yourself becoming more and more deeply relaxed with every breath. Allow the sensation of relaxation to wash over your entire body. When you are deeply relaxed you are ready to begin the visualisation.

It is your serve. Imagine yourself standing at the baseline. Your opponent is at the other side of the net, ready to receive. Visualise yourself preparing to serve. Watch yourself bouncing the ball—one bounce, two bounces, three bounces—until you are relaxed and ready to serve. Take a slow, deep breath. Visualise the exact spot in your opponent's service box where your serve is going to land.

See yourself tossing the ball—high and smooth, just in front of you. Watch as your knees bend. Imagine the swing as you take the racquet back behind your back and then up and out in front of you, reaching high and in front to connect with the ball. Imagine making a perfect connection with the ball as your body, arm and racquet are in alignment. Hear the sound of the ball hitting the strings and the 'whoosh' as the ball rushes through the air and hits the exact perfect spot you had imagined. See your opponent rooted to the spot as the ball screams past them.

BEHAVIOURAL TECHNIQUES

CHAPTER EIGHT
Behavioural Strategies

Chapter Objectives

After reading this chapter you will be able to describe:

Why preparation is so important
Why sleep & diet are important
Negative & positive body language

After reading this chapter you will know how to:

Get a good night's sleep
Eat the right kind of diet
Make a preparation checklist
Avoid gamesmanship
Use positive body language

Preparation

Adequate pre-match preparation will mean that you are not unnecessarily stressed by matters off the court, allowing you to focus your mind and body on the actual match. Preparation includes making sure that you have a good night's sleep, eating and drinking sensibly and avoiding foods or beverages which might exacerbate anxiety in your body, and ensuring that you have all the necessary equipment for the task at hand—the match.

Sleep

Anxiety interferes with sleep—how many times have you lain awake at night with worrying thoughts running through your mind? Lack of sleep interferes with your ability to remain alert during the day and can cause your on-court reactions to become dull and slow. A good night's sleep is essential preparation to play to the best of one's abilities. Below are a series of tips for maximising your chances of a restful night's sleep.

1. Do some exercise each day—but not too close to bedtime, as this will make your mind and body too alert.

2. Avoid naps of more than 10 or 15-minutes duration during the day so that you will be tired at bedtime.

3. Develop a 'sleep ritual' or bedtime routine in order to send the right messages to your body and brain that you are about to wind down and sleep. For example, have a warm bath to relax your body—but avoid showering because this is too stimulating; and try and set a regular bedtime and waking-up time—even at weekends—in order to allow your body's internal clock to regulate itself to a stable pattern.

4. Try and sleep in the same bedroom and the same bed every night and reserve the bed for sleeping and sex only. Don't use it for other activities such as paperwork or exercise—these will only send mixed messages to your subconscious mind.

5. Allow enough time in bed for around 8-hours sleep a night in order to be fully rested for the day ahead.

6. Create a 'sleep-conducive environment' which includes a comfortable mattress and pillows in a darkened, quiet room, free from distractions—keep distractions such as televisions and computers out of the bedroom. Keep the temperature cool rather than cold or too hot.

7. Watch what you eat: avoid eating a heavy meal in the hours before bedtime; avoid spicy food or foods high in tyramine, such as cheese, bacon, nuts and soy sauce, all of which trigger the release of norepinephrine, which is a neuro-stimulant. Instead, eat foods such as bread or cereal which trigger the release of serotonin—another neurotransmitter which helps make us sleepy.

8. Watch what you drink: avoid alcohol—it is a diuretic and will make you get up several times during the night to go to the toilet; and avoid caffeine—a stimulant. Instead, try drinking milk—this contains tryptophan, which triggers the release of serotonin and helps slows down brain activity.

9. Avoid nicotine—that is also a stimulant.

10. If you have trouble getting off to sleep, do some breathing exercises to relax your body and mind; do your relaxation techniques or use a relaxation/sleep tape—there are several commercially available.

11. Don't clock-watch and if you must get up in the night, do something boring such as reading a dull book—avoid doing anything that might stimulate your brain.

Sleep Tips

'DO'	'DON'T'
Light exercise during the day	Nap too often/long
Have a warm bath	Shower
Set a regular bed and waking time	Have distractions in the bedroom
Sleep in the same room	Work in the room
Get a good 8 hours	Eat a heavy/spicy meal
Eat cereal or bread	Drink coffee/tea
Drink milk	Smoke
Breathing/relaxation exercises	Clock watch

Diet

Diet can affect how we feel; certain foods can make us more or less anxious, typically by triggering certain chemicals in the body that influence the activity of the neurotransmitters and the autonomic nervous system.

Before matches, it is best to avoid certain foods, including those with a high sugar content (e.g. sweets and cakes) or those containing refined carbohydrates (e.g. white bread). These kinds of foods can create an imbalance in the blood-sugar levels and exacerbate anxiety. Too much sugar produces a condition known as hypoglycaemia, which produces symptoms very similar to those experienced in an anxiety state. It is best to eat a healthy, balanced diet, containing vegetables, fruit and whole grains.

Likewise, it is best to avoid certain drinks before a game, particularly coffee or other drinks containing caffeine (including tea and some soft drinks). Coffee blocks certain neuro-transmitters in the brain and is the most widely used mood altering drug in the world. It enhances alertness, concentration and memory and is therefore a stimulant; but too much can produce over-stimulation, especially if one is susceptible or has an already over-stimulated nervous system. In experimental studies, caffeine has been shown to induce panic-attacks, exacerbate stress and anxiety. It stimulates the body's secretion of insulin, which lowers blood sugar, for which the body compensates by releasing adrenaline. Caffeine withdrawal has also been shown to trigger muscle pains, irritability and anxiety.

Diet Tips

EAT/DRINK	AVOID
Fruit	Sweets/cakes
Nuts	Refined carbohydrates
Vegetables	Coffee
Whole grains	Tea
Milk	Fizzy drinks
Water	Foods rich in tyramine

The Racquet Bag

It goes without saying that you should take to the match in your bag everything that is necessary to play, including your racquet and a spare racquet (if you have one), all the necessary kit including the appropriate shoes for the court surface and spare laces, running first aid equipment such as plasters, a change of kit, a towel, water or a sports drink and perhaps some high-energy snacks. Check your bag before you leave to make sure you have everything that you need.

Arrival & Game Plan

Arrive at the club in plenty of time as rushing at the last minute will cause unnecessary amounts of adrenaline to pump through your body. If possible, exercise prior to going on court by gentle stretching and other exercises to warm up your muscles, heart and lungs.

Have a game plan. Have at least an 'A' and 'B' plan. If you know your opponent and have played them before, this will give you an advantage in your preparation, so before you arrive at the match, think about your game plan—why not write it down on a piece of paper?

If you don't know your opponent, before the match think about how you might play against different styles; quickly identify your opponent's strengths and weaknesses in the warm-up and during the early games. The most basic advice is to avoid their strengths whilst playing to their weaknesses; and play to your strengths whilst trying to avoid letting your opponent play to your weaknesses.

Preparation Checklist

Bag	Game Plan
Racquets	Plan 'A'
Shoes	Plan 'B'
Laces	Paper
Towel	Pen
First Aid	
Fluid	
Snacks	

Gamesmanship

Gamesmanship is defined as the art of winning without actually cheating but by deliberately attempting to put your opponent off his/her game. Gamesmanship occurs in both overt or crude ways as well as more subtle, difficult to detect ways. Gamesmanship occurs before, during and after the match.

Before the match, your opponent may use gamesmanship to make a host of excuses as to why they are unlikely to play well that day—they've had a late night, have various aches and pains, haven't been playing well lately. All these excuses may serve in part to prepare them for failure—if you beat them they can blame their defeat on a bad knee or some other problem. However, if you are anxious they may serve to make you even more anxious by raising your expectation of winning—and therefore heightening your fear of failure.

Sometimes, people use gamesmanship in the opposite way prior to the match—to tell you how well they are playing, how many tournaments they have won and who they have beaten lately. Some opponents will enquire about the other games you've played in the league or ladder and like to tell you about how easily they beat an opponent you lost to or struggled to beat—in that way undermining your confidence and instilling in you the expectation of being beaten even before a ball has been hit.

During the game, some opponents will use gamesmanship to put you off your own game. Sometimes this takes the form of a compliment about your style of play which can serve to draw your attention to something you had been doing automatically and without much conscious thought to that point. Sometimes, particularly with a motor skill, conscious thought inhibits performance. For example, telling you how well you are serving may have the effect of breaking down your serve.

Sometimes during the match an opponent might try to engage you in conversation in order to distract you from your own concentration and focus. They may try to speed up the match or slow it down, depending on the ebb and flow of the points and who was winning at any particular time—typically speeding it up when they are winning and trying to slow it down when you are on top. They may make comments to you at the changeover between games to distract or upset you.

After the match, particularly if they have lost, their excuses may role from their tongue at a rate of knots, complaining about their physical health, the state of their equipment, the weather, distractions from other players, good or bad luck—good for you and bad for them!—comments about the age difference between you or the amount of practice you have been doing compared to the fact that they have seldom played of late.

Coping with gamesmanship and not allowing it to bother you, upset you or put you off your game is a real skill. The best thing is to ignore it as much as you can. Certainly, don't get drawn into a battle of gamesmanship—the competition is on the court not in the conversation between you. Certainly, never allow your opponent to see that they have angered you or made you feel anxious—simply do not react to things they do or say. At all times, keep calm and draw upon the many techniques you will have learned from reading this book and from practising your psychological coping skills off and on the court. Remember, the reason why people use gamesmanship is because their actual play is not good enough. Remember that tennis is a sport played on a court but a game played in the mind.

Body Language

Body language is any behaviour or communication that is not verbal or spoken aloud. Social psychologists have found that less than 10% of the messages we convey to others are in words; more that 90% of our communications are non-verbal through our tone of voice, eye contact, posture, hand gestures, movements and facial expressions.

Where there is a mismatch between what a person says in their words and their body language whilst they are speaking, we tend to place more emphasis on their non-spoken communication than on what they are saying. This is because people have less conscious control over their body language than their spoken language—meaning that if we can read our opponent's body language then we can read their true feelings.

Negative body language

Negative body language which signals nervousness includes clearing the throat, fidgeting and wringing of hands. Negative body language which signals anger includes a tightened jaw, arms folded across the chest, intense eye contact, tightened muscles, hunched shoulders, shallow breathing and clenched fists, holding the head in the palm of the hands, 'tutting' sounds, running your hand through your hair, rubbing the back of your neck, kicking at the ground or at an imaginary object.

During a match, avoid all of these negative body language signals, particularly slumped shoulders, dropping your head, looking to the sky in despair, vicious or angry swipes of your racquet after making a mistake or miss-hit, wildly hitting at balls between points in annoyance, making 'tutting' or similar sounds—all of these non-verbal behaviours let your opponent know that he or she is getting under your skin. Knowing this will increase their motivation whilst your motivation is either in decline or so high that you are losing control. In his autobiography, Boris Becker made it clear that once he saw an opponent's shoulders slump, he knew that their resolve had been broken and at that point he would step up his game in order to take advantage and win.

In many ways, negative body language is similar to the kinds of negative self-talk problems discussed earlier in that they set up a vicious cycle of despair and hopelessness, leading ultimately to defeat. Being able to read your opponent's body language will give you a quick snapshot of how they are feeling and whether they are in control or losing confidence.

Positive body language

In sport as in life, it is important to show a positive mental attitude or 'PMA'—don't let your opponent see that you look defeated; don't let them know that fantastic winner you just hit was actually a mistake and went in a different area of the court from that which you aimed; don't let them know that the net court they just won a point on irritated or upset you.

Keep your body language positive at all times, even if it does not match with how you feel inside—stand tall, hold your head high, don't grimace or scowl. Hold your head up and shoulders back and walk confidently. Positive body language includes a strong, firm handshake when meeting your opponent. Lean forward, give them some eye contact and a smile. Show them that you are confident and secure in yourself and therefore in your ability.

Body Language

Positive	Negative
Stand tall	Hunched shoulders
Head high	Shallow breathing
Shoulders back	Clenched fist
Walk confident	Dropped head
Eye-contact	Looking to the sky
Firm handshake	Hitting at balls wildly
Smile	Tutting
	Sighing

CHAPTER NINE
Coping with pressure & anxiety

Chapter Objectives

After reading this chapter you will be able to describe:

How to cope with pressure & anxiety

After reading this chapter you will know how to:

Use the PRESSURE model of coping

Coping with pressure and anxiety is not unique to club players; elite athletes experience very similar feelings—the majority of sports psychology consultations for high level professional athletes are in relation to helping them manage their anxiety levels.

How we interpret situations in our minds may be more important than the objective importance of the actual competition. Consequently, those high in trait anxiety and of low self-esteem are likely to generate more worrying thoughts and have higher levels of somatic anxiety that will interfere with their performance, regardless of the situation in which they find themselves. The other side of the same coin is that high levels of self-confidence—that is a belief in our own ability to succeed—have been shown to guard against cognitive anxiety and worrying thoughts and help performance.

Having read this book, you will now realise that anxiety and stress are universal, part of everyday life, and that to be anxious is to be human. You will understand how anxiety can be a helpful emotion—especially if it motivates you to train harder and play better tennis.

You will have a good appreciation of how anxiety can change our bodies, influence the ways in which we think and determine how we behave on and off court as these three systems—the somatic, cognitive and behavioural—interact in a vicious cycle such that when somatic and cognitive anxiety are excessive they will inhibit performance. You will also recognise how the way we feel on court is determined by our personalities and the situations in which we find ourselves—for example, how important we perceive an event to be, the degree of uncertainty to which we are exposed, the level of skill we possess and whether or not we are exposed to an audience.

Having read and hopefully re-read aspects of this book, you will be familiar with a host of skills and techniques to help manage your anxiety on and off court. You will have practiced the somatic techniques of deep breathing and progressive relaxation. You will have tested out some cognitive skills, such as distraction, positive self-talk and visualisation, and you will be adept at self-monitoring and conducting behavioural experiments to test out your ideas. You will know how to prepare for competition by managing your sleep routine and diet and making sure that you have an arrival and game plan. You will know how to avoid becoming a victim of your opponent's gamesmanship and you will be able to exude positive body language and self-belief.

PRESSURE

I wish to conclude by offering you the advice of Butler (1996), who proposed the use of 'PRESSURE' as a mnemonic to help cope with competitive sporting occasions:

PREPARE	prepare psychologically for competition
RELAX	use breathing exercises to prevent over arousal
EXTERNALISE	locate the problem outside yourself in order to reduce pressure
STAY POSITIVE	have confidence in your ability
SINGLE-MINDED	stay task focused in training and in competition
UNITE	at doubles in tennis work together as a team
RE-EVALUATE	how important is this match in the bigger scheme of things?
EXTEND YOURSELF	try your best no matter how important, or equally unimportant, the competition is.

ISBN 142512080-6

Edwards Brothers Malloy
Oxnard, CA USA
August 19, 2014